Finding Christ's Church

WITH MAPS TO SHOW THE WAY

by

John A. O'Brien, Ph.D., LL.D.

University of Notre Dame

With a Foreword by

The Most Rev. John F. Noll, D.D.

Archbishop-Bishop of Fort Wayne

*Ask, and it shall be given to you: seek and you
shall find: knock, and it shall be opened unto you.*
Christ's Sermon on the Mount. *Matthew* 7:7

AVE MARIA PRESS

Notre Dame, Indiana 46556

NIHIL OBSTAT

Felix D. Duffey, C.S.C.
Censor Deputatus

IMPRIMATUR

✠ Most Rev. John F. Noll, D.D.
Archbishop-Bishop of Fort Wayne

Revised edition — Second printing, March, 1968

FOREWORD

THIS is another among many excellent books of instruction written by Reverend John A. O'Brien, Ph.D., of the philosophy of religion at the University of Notre Dame. It is not to be adjudged the least of the products of his pen, however, because of its smaller size. More literature is brought into every home today than its members take time to read. Hence books on religious and spiritual subjects have a better chance of perusal if they present their message briefly.

Indeed, the brevity and conciseness with which the author presents a subject of vast importance will win a greater multitude of readers; for this book is a capital illustration of the old Latin phrase, *multum in parvo*—much in little space. It deserves millions of readers.

Millions of Americans refrain even from beginning to investigate Christ's way of salvation because the many, who pose as experts in explaining His way, speak so discordantly. Yet if man has an eternal destiny, God must have provided a sure way of reaching it. For fifteen centuries all Christians felt convinced that they knew this way, and that if they were not treading it, it was their own fault.

Today it is not so. Scarcely twenty-five per cent of our population would insist that "they know the truth." Another twenty-five per cent would maintain that each person may read into his Guidebook—the Bible—the way which best satisfies his own inclinations or preferences. The other fifty per cent either have never striven to learn whether there is a divinely appointed way of salvation, or they have actually striven not to find out lest their consciences become disturbed.

Father O'Brien shows with convincing evidence that God did

establish a way. To enable you to find that way, the author has mapped it out carefully and has established signposts along the way. If you will follow those signs, you will not be led astray; for you will be traveling along God's highway.

The undersigned requests you to study the author's maps prayerfully, and assures you in return that "peace in believing," which follows compliance with the Creator's requirements.

✠ Most Rev. John F. Noll, D.D.

Archbishop-Bishop of Fort Wayne

CONTENTS

Chapter 1
CLEARING THE WAY

ALL persons have a goal in life. For some, it is advancement in their chosen line of work. For others, it is the building of a happy home, the amassing of riches, the gaining of political influence, the achieving of social prominence and popularity.

Though these objectives may differ widely, there is one goal that all people have in common. It is the salvation of one's soul, the attainment of everlasting life, the achieving of the ultimate end for which every human being has been created by God.

If that end is achieved, life has been a glorious success; if that great goal is not maintained, life has been a tragic failure. The loss is irreparable: no amount of success in business, in one's profession, in society or in politics, can retrieve that failure.

On the other hand, if life's supreme objective is attained, no matter how poor one is, or how little success he achieved in business, or how little prominence he gained in society, life is an unqualified success. He has gained the only victory that really matters: the saving of his immortal soul.

In stating this, the writer is expressing not merely his private opinion but the truth uttered with such impressive solemnity by the divine Master, Jesus Christ, when He said: "For what shall it profit a man, if he gain the whole world, and suffer the loss of his soul?" (Mark 8:36). That is the central truth in the teaching of Jesus; it is the point of emphasis in every Christian Church. Differ though they may on other matters, Christian Churches are all in agreement upon the clear teaching of Jesus that the saving of one's soul is more important than the gaining of the whole world.

A PRACTICAL QUESTION

But you will ask—and rightly: "How is one to achieve that goal? I am convinced, as are practically all the people of America . . . and indeed the whole civilized world . . . that the attainment of everlasting life with God in heaven is man's ultimate end and his supreme goal. But what I want to know is, *how* can I reach that goal? What are the *means* which I am to use to achieve it? What is the good of emphasizing the importance of the objective if specific directions are not given to enable me to attain it?"

You are right; that is the *practical* question. It is the question which we now proceed to answer. The answer which we give is that which Christ gave and which we unhesitatingly accept; because of its importance, the question requires a full and detailed reply which will admit of no misunderstanding.

Before presenting it, may we ask you to follow the presentation with an *open* mind and an eye single to the truths laid down by Christ. If you divest yourself of all preconceived notions and prejudices and enter into the discussion with eagerness to learn the truth and a humble willingness to follow it whithersoever it may lead you, you will derive the greatest profit. Should we not all accept the clear teachings of Jesus with the simplicity, the humility and the docility of a little child? Listen to the words of Christ:

"And Jesus calling unto him a little child, set him in the midst of them, and said: Amen I say to you, unless you be converted, and become as little children, you shall not enter into the kingdom of heaven: Whosoever therefore shall humble himself as this little child, he is the greater in the kingdom of heaven" (Matthew 18:2-4).

Such is the model for all who seek to know the teachings of Christ and the directions which He gave for the attainment of man's supreme goal—the kingdom of heaven. An attitude of open-mindedness, of humility, of prayerfulness, of childlike docility to the revealed word of God will bring you the greatest dividends both in time and in eternity.

KINDNESS AND GOOD WILL

Having asked that from you, we promise in return that we shall not deviate in our presentation by a hair's breadth from the clear teachings of the divine Founder of the Christian faith. On our part

8

we bring to the discussion a respectful adherence to the word of God and a heart full of good will and love for you.

As the writer is a stranger to you, perhaps it may not be inappropriate to say that he is no narrow-minded sectarian who thinks that all who believe otherwise, however honestly, have a one-way ticket to the nethermost regions. If he were a person of such a stripe, he would not have been invited to speak on the Catholic faith in the leading Protestant Churches — Methodist Episcopal, Presbyterian, Congregational, Disciples of Christ, Lutheran and Episcopalian—of the community in which he ministered for nearly a quarter of a century. Neither would he have received from the Acacia fraternity, composed exclusively of Masons, a gold Knights of Columbus pin as a token of their appreciation of the influence for friendship and good will which they esteem he exercised among students and faculty of all faiths at the University of Illinois campus.

For nearly a quarter of a century the writer taught university students of all faiths, including ministers of various Protestant denominations, the philosophy of religion and the basic truths of Christianity and mingled with all of them in friendly intimacy. He has spent more than 40 years at the universities of Illinois, Oxford and Notre Dame, engrossed in the philosophy of religion, whose major task is to supply a correct answer to the question in the minds of millions of thoughtful men and women today: What are the means which God has provided, and which He wishes me to use, to achieve my eternal salvation?

The writer mentions these facts in an objective manner, with no thought of vainglory but simply that you may believe him when he tells you that this exposition of Christ's teaching comes to you from a heart full of friendship and love for you. Now for the task at hand.

CHRIST'S PLAN

Christ did not fail to provide a safe guide for man in the quest for eternal life. He did not allow every individual to sink or swim in accordance with his own ingenuity in finding out for himself every step of the path that leads to man's heavenly home: that would have meant the loss of the vast majority.

Christ established a definite institution, clothed it with the power and authority to teach all men His truths, to sanctify them, and to assist them at every step of the way in the saving of their souls. That institution is the Church He founded: the holy, Catholic, Apostolic Church, governed by St. Peter and his successors from the days of Christ down to the present time. In consequence, Christ wishes, nay commands, that every child of Adam embrace that faith and avail himself of the Church's authoritative teaching and un-erring guidance.

There are many persons, of course, who do not believe that Christ founded a visible, organized institution as His Church. Others dispute the Catholic Church's claims to be that institution. We do not question the sincerity of those who, in good faith, do not agree with us. We wish merely to discuss here the chief reasons given for not embracing the Catholic Church as the divinely established Church. These reasons have generally taken three forms:

1. All religions are equally good and true; therefore, it doesn't really matter which Church you choose to attend.

2. Sincerity is what counts with God; believe in any religion, attend any Church; as long as you are sincere, you are all right and will be saved.

3. Christ gave us the Bible: we take our own religion from the Bible; therefore, we need no Church to guide us in our belief or in our conduct.

Have you not heard one or another or all these statements? In fact, they are in the very air we breathe; we hear them on all sides; we think we have encountered them in one form or another a thousand times.

"IT DOESN'T MATTER . . ."

Let us now consider the first of these claims: it doesn't matter what creed a man believes, what Church he embraces. First of all, we distinguish between that proposition as an expression of the emotions and as an assertion of the intellect. As an expression of the emotions, it is intended to reflect kindliness and good will. With that sentiment of friendliness we do not wish to quarrel; it is the kindly sentiment which is implied in the assertion that has been chiefly responsible for its wide currency. That, plus the fact that it ministers to man's natural indolence and spares him from the painstaking task of finding out which Church is the true one.

As an expression of the intellect, the claim of the indifferentist is wholly untenable. Why? Because it violates the first principles of logic and is in obvious opposition to the clear teachings of Jesus. It is a simple dictate of logic and of common sense that contradictory statements cannot both be right: if one is right, then the other *must* be wrong. We recognize this in the affairs of our daily life and would consign to a sanitarium the individual who reasoned and acted otherwise.

To illustrate. A teacher takes a piece of white chalk and writes on the blackboard. She asks eight members of her class, "What is the color of that writing?" One answers, "purple"; another, "green"; another, "red"; another "yellow." Still another replies, "violet"; another, "orange"; another, "black." Finally the eighth pupil says: "Why, that's white . . . and no mistake about it."

The teacher loves all of her pupils equally. Let us suppose she says: "You are all equally correct." Then with one hand she clasps the hand of the pupil who said it was black, and with the other she clasps the hand of the student who said it was white, and beaming upon each of them, observes: "Both equally right, my dears!"

What would you think of such a performance? Would you not say, "The teacher has a big heart all right, but . . . a soft head. She can satisfy her desire to agree with all of them only at the expense of intellectual suicide. The student who said it was *white* was right; all the others were wrong: that is the long and the short of it"?

CONDEMNED BY TWO COURTS

Now let us apply this line of reasoning to differences in religious belief. We ask: "Was Christ divine or was He merely a man?" The

Unitarian replies: "Merely a man." The Methodist answers: "Christ was divine." Can we shake the hands of each and say: "You are both equally correct"? Not without destroying all possibility of correct human reasoning. Yet differences similar to the foregoing exist among all the various creeds and Churches. Therefore common sense demands that we reject the assertion of the religious indifferentist . . . among other reasons, to protect the sanity of the human mind. His assertion stands condemned before the court of human reason.

Religious indifferentism stands equally condemned before the bar of divine revelation. On trial for His life before Caiphas, Jesus gave no countenance to the claim of the indifferentist. "I adjure Thee by the living God," said the high priest, "that Thou tell us if Thou be Christ the Son of God" (Matthew 26:63).

Jesus knew that His life hung upon His answer: He could escape by denying His divinity; but He never faltered. Without hesitation, Jesus replied in the affirmative, saying. "Thou hast said it." Thus did He seal His fate and go to His death upon Calvary's Cross rather than give a misleading answer.

His command to the Apostles displays equal scorn for the indifferentist: "Going therefore, teach ye all nations . . . teaching them to observe *all things whatsoever* I have commanded you . . ." The Apostles understood clearly that neither they nor the faithful were to depart one iota from the teachings which Christ commanded them to impart. St. Paul declares: "But though . . . an angel from heaven, preach a gospel to you besides that which we have preached to you, let him be anathema" (Galatians 1:8). Thus do the teachings of Christ and the Apostles repudiate the claim of the religious indifferentist.

SINCERITY IS NOT ENOUGH

Let us consider now the second reason offered for failing to comply with Christ's command to believe His teachings under pain of eternal condemnation. "He that believeth and is baptized," said Christ, "shall be saved: but he that believeth not shall be con-

12

demned" (Mark 16:16). This second theory asserts that as long as a person is sincere in believing, that is all that matters: under this pretext the most fantastic and bizarre doctrines would be justified. Here again we make a distinction between sincerity as a subjective quality, an attitude of the mind, and as a substitute for objective truth and for reasonable efforts to find it.

Sincerity, as a subjective quality, like the sentiment of good will and friendliness in the attitude of the religious indifferentist, is very commonly respected. But sincerity, like good will, must have eyes; it must be directed by intelligence; otherwise it will be led by blind emotion and serve merely to bolster falsehood. Sincerity, however, *as a substitute for objective truth and for reasonable efforts to discover it,* in the sense in which it is used by the religious indifferentist, is wrong and worthy only of condemnation.

To illustrate. Let us suppose the reader is ill; the doctor has prescribed some medicine which is in a glass near the bed. Beside that glass is another filled with poison, which the nurse uses to disinfect her hands. She comes into your room at midnight; she does not know for certain which is the medicine and which is the poison. Suppose she says to herself: "I don't know which is which, but I think this is the medicine; I'm sincere about it and that is enough."

Accordingly, she gives you the glass containing the poison and you get worse at once and are brought to death's door.

Would any amount of sincerity on her part excuse her from the duty of using her intelligence to find out the truth? Does not sincerity imply the duty of doing all in one's power to discover the truth and to act accordingly? Would you not say that such a nurse is exceedingly culpable because she failed to make an effort to discover the objective fact: which glass contained the medicine and which the poison? Without depreciating the virtue of sincerity, would you not feel compelled to say: "Sincerity is an admirable virtue, but it must not be used as a substitute for truth, nor as an excuse for not making every reasonable effort to ascertain the truth"?

WOULD YOU DO THIS?

If you had a Swiss watch to be repaired, would you take it to a blacksmith and accept his sincerity in place of skill to repair it? If you had a legal matter of great complexity, would you take it to a sincere carpenter and accept his sincerity in lieu of knowledge to guide you through the technicalities of the law? If you were taken critically ill, would you call in a sincere bricklayer and accept his sincerity in place of medical knowledge to effect your recovery? No, you would not belittle the virtue of sincerity but you would say that it must never be used as a *substitute* for knowledge nor as an *excuse* for not making an intelligent effort to secure that knowledge.

Such is the position of the Catholic Church. She respects sincerity as highly as any other organization in the world: she merely asks that a person *prove* his sincerity by making a careful investigation to discover which is the Church founded by Christ for the salvation of all mankind. If a person makes such an investigation honestly and thoroughly, and at the outset divests his mind of prejudice, the objective evidence is so clear and unmistakable that he can scarcely fail to find the true Church. The entrance of nearly *two million* converts to the Catholic Church in the United States in the 25-year period between 1926 and 1951 offers abundant evidence of this fact.

If, however, because of prejudices which he cannot eradicate or because of other circumstances beyond his control, he does not find the true faith of Christ but believes in his own creed with sincerity and good faith, then he is not culpable in the eyes of God. Here is a case where sincerity is proved through earnest and reasonable effort to find the objective truth.

This is the clear teaching of Pope Pius IX, who in 1854 and 1863 declared: "We must . . . recognize with certainty that those who are in invincible ignorance of the true religion are not guilty of this in the eyes of God . . . and may, aided by the light of divine grace, attain to eternal life. God . . . by no means permits that anyone suffer eternal punishment who has not of his own free will fallen into sin . . . And who will presume to mark out the limits of this ignorance and diversity of peoples, countries, minds and the rest?"

Reflecting the infallible teaching of the Supreme Pontiff, the Baltimore Catechism says: "They who remain outside the Catholic Church through no grave fault of their own and do not know it is the true Church, can be saved by making use of the graces which God gives them. Those who are outside the Church through no fault of their own are not culpable in the sight of God because of their invincible ignorance."

CHURCH IS BROAD-MINDED

The broad-mindedness and maternal solicitude of the Church for the salvation of all mankind are nowhere more strikingly apparent than in this teaching. Most non-Catholics express astonishment upon learning of the Church's teaching on this subject. "Why," they say, "we were under the impression that your Church teaches that only her own actual members can possibly be saved . . . that there is no chance for Protestants and others outside her fold. Your explanation has given us a new insight into the mind of your Church; certainly nothing could be fairer, more broad-minded, more reasonable, than the teaching you have just explained to us."

Yes, contrary to the impression of many outside her fold, the Catholic Church is the most broad-minded—in the best sense of that term—and the most reasonable institution in the world. As an organization reflecting the mind of Christ and perpetuating His teachings, she would be bound to be the last word in kindliness and in reasonableness. Though she opposes every heresy, as Christ obliges her to do, she loves the heretic: though she fights sin with all her power and resourcefulness, she loves the sinner and never despairs of winning him to a life of virtue and holiness. She holds ajar the door of salvation for every human being; only he who acts contrary to the light of his own conscience and who refuses to investigate if he doubts closes that door upon himself.

BIBLE ALONE SUFFICIENT?

We come now to the third reason which people assign for not

15

CHART I

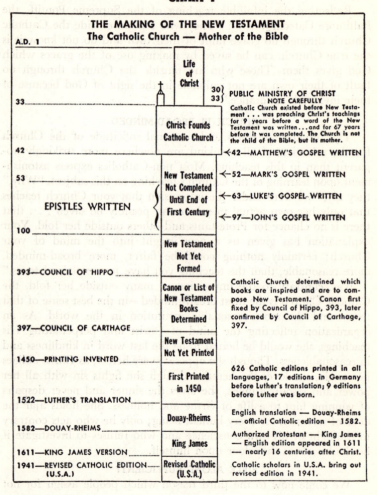

THE MAKING OF THE NEW TESTAMENT
The Catholic Church — Mother of the Bible

A.D. 1

Life of Christ

30
33

33

PUBLIC MINISTRY OF CHRIST
NOTE CAREFULLY
Catholic Church existed before New Testament . . . was preaching Christ's teachings for 9 years before a word of the New Testament was written . . . and for 67 years before it was completed. The Church is not the child of the Bible, but its mother.

Christ Founds Catholic Church

42 ← 42—MATTHEW'S GOSPEL WRITTEN

53 **New Testament Not Completed Until End of First Century** ← 52—MARK'S GOSPEL WRITTEN

EPISTLES WRITTEN ← 63—LUKE'S GOSPEL WRITTEN

← 97—JOHN'S GOSPEL WRITTEN

100

New Testament Not Yet Formed

393—COUNCIL OF HIPPO

Canon or List of New Testament Books Determined

Catholic Church determined which books are inspired and are to compose New Testament. Canon first fixed by Council of Hippo, 393, later confirmed by Council of Carthage, 397.

397—COUNCIL OF CARTHAGE

New Testament Not Yet Printed

1450—PRINTING INVENTED

First Printed in 1450

626 Catholic editions printed in all languages, 17 editions in Germany before Luther's translation; 9 editions before Luther was born.

1522—LUTHER'S TRANSLATION

Douay-Rheims

English translation — Douay-Rheims — official Catholic edition — 1582.

1582—DOUAY-RHEIMS

King James

Authorized Protestant — King James — English edition appeared in 1611 — nearly 16 centuries after Christ.

1611—KING JAMES VERSION

1941—REVISED CATHOLIC EDITION (U.S.A.)

Revised Catholic (U.S.A.)

Catholic scholars in U.S.A. bring out revised edition in 1941.

16

being members of the Church founded by Christ to guide and assist them in the attainment of eternal life: the claim that they have the Bible, get their religion directly from it, and do not need the Church to guide them. How often have we heard a non-Catholic friend say: "I'm a Bible Christian. I get my religion from it without consulting any priest."

The fact is, however, that not one in a hundred such persons has any accurate understanding of the origin of the Bible, particularly of the New Testament which is of supreme importance for Christians. They seem to think that the New Testament existed before the Church and that the latter is its creature, coming into existence in the centuries following the preaching of the word of God. To correct the many erroneous impressions which well-meaning and even devout people have on this subject, we have prepared a chart presenting in outline form the story of how the New Testament came into being.

That chart, *The Making of the New Testament,* will repay careful study.

Explanation of the Chart: This chart presents in outline form the essential historical facts about the origin and formation of the New Testament. In showing how it came into being, the chart shows that it owes its existence to the Catholic Church, the Mother of the Bible.

The chart likewise brings into clear relief the following important facts:

1. The New Testament was written in its entirety by Catholics.

2. St. Peter, the first Pope of the Catholic Church, is the author of two of its epistles.

3. The Catholic Church determined the canon or list of books to constitute the New Testament.

4. The declaration of the Catholic Church that the books of the New Testament are all inspired by God constitutes the *sole* authority for the universal belief of both Catholics and Protestants in their inspired character.

17

5. The Catholic Church existed before the New Testament.

6. The Catholic Church is the Mother of the New Testament.

If she had not scrutinized carefully the writings of her children, rejecting some and approving others as worthy of inclusion in the canon of the New Testament, there would be no New Testament today.

If she had not declared the books composing the New Testament to be the inspired word of God, we would not know it.

The only authority which non-Catholics have for the inspiration of the Scriptures is the authority of the Catholic Church. If the latter be rejected, there remain no logical grounds for retention of the cardinal tenet of all Protestants—the inspired character of Scripture.

With the possible exception of St. John, none of the Apostles ever saw all the writings which now make up the New Testament.

MOTHER OF THE BIBLE

If the Church did not preserve the Bible, shielding it from the attacks of barbarians, copying it in her monasteries throughout the long centuries before printing was invented, the modern world would be without a Bible.

The chart shows that the Catholic Church, founded by Jesus Christ, was teaching and preaching the word of God nine years before a word of the New Testament was written and for 67 years before it was completed. The truths enunciated by her divine Founder were deep in her heart and fresh in her memory; she was busily engaged in imparting these orally to mankind.

Christ wrote nothing; neither did He command the Apostles to write. He commissioned them to teach His doctrines to all mankind. "Go ye into the whole world," He said, "and preach the gospel to every creature." The Apostles fulfilled the command of Christ by their oral preaching.

Peter, Matthew, John, James and Jude supplemented their preaching by writing. It is well to remember, however, that the Church was a *going concern,* a functioning institution, teaching,

18

preaching, administering the sacraments, saving souls, before the New Testament ever saw the light of day.

She is not the child of the Bible, as many non-Catholics imagine, but its Mother. She derives neither her existence nor her teaching authority from the New Testament; she had both before the New Testament was born; she secured her being, her teachings, her authority directly from Jesus Christ.

If all the books of the Bible and all the copies were blotted out, she would still be in possession of all the truths of Christ and could still continue to preach them as she did before a single word of the New Testament was written. For those truths are deep in her mind, heart and memory, in her liturgical and sacramental life, in the traditions, written and unwritten, which go directly back to Christ.

Great as is our reverence for the Bible, reason and experience compel us to say that it alone is not a competent nor a safe guide as to what we are to believe. A competent guide for the Christian religion must possess these three qualifications:

1. It must be within the reach of every inquirer after truth.

2. It must be clear and intelligible to all.

3. It must present all the truths of the Christian religion.

The Bible, however, possesses none of these qualifications.

NOT ACCESSIBLE TO ALL

First, the Scriptures were not accessible to the primitive Christians. Since the New Testament was not completed till near the end of the first century, it was obviously not available to those who died before that time. Neither was it accessible to the Christians for the *first four* centuries since the canon or list of 27 books to comprise the New Testament was not determined by the Church till 393. Furthermore, it was not available from the *fourth to the fifteenth century* because the printing press was not invented until about 1440 and hence it was impossible to provide each member with a copy. Even at the present time, as in all previous ages, there are millions who are unable to read, millions to whom the Bible remains a sealed Book.

19

Secondly, the Bible is not a clear and intelligible guide to all. There are many passages in the Bible which are difficult and obscure, not only to the ordinary person but to the highly trained scholar as well. St. Peter himself tells us that in the Epistles of St. Paul there are "certain things hard to be understood, which the unlearned and unstable wrest, as they do also the other scriptures, to their own destruction" (2 Peter 3:16). Consequently, he tells us elsewhere "that no prophecy of the scripture is made by private interpretation" (2 Peter 1:20).

St. Luke narrates in the Acts of the Apostles that a certain man was riding in his chariot, reading the Book of Isaias. Upon being asked by St. Philip whether he understood the meaning of the prophecy, he replied: "How can I understand unless some man show me?" In these modest words is reflected the experience of practically all readers of the Bible. True, in the first years of his separation from the Church, Luther declared that the Bible could be interpreted by everyone, "even by a humble miller's maid, nay by a child of nine." Later on, however, when the Anabaptists, the Zwinglians and others contradicted his views, the Bible became "a heresy book," most obscure and difficult to understand. He lived to see numerous heretical sects rise up and spread through Christendom, all claiming to be based upon the Bible.

Thus, in 1525, he sadly deplored the religious anarchy to which his own principle of the private interpretation of Scripture had given rise: "There are as many sects and beliefs as there are heads. This fellow will have nothing to do with baptism; another denies the Sacrament; a third believes that there is another world between this and the Last Day. Some teach that Christ is not God; some say this, some that. There is no rustic so rude but that, if he dreams or fancies anything, it must be the whisper of the Holy Ghost, and he himself a prophet."[1]

The hundreds of bickering sects all claiming to draw their doc-

---

1. Grisar, *Luther IV*, 386-407.

trines from the Bible offer abundant evidence that the Bible alone is not a clear and a safe guide.

DOES NOT CONTAIN ALL TEACHINGS

Thirdly, the Bible does not contain *all* the teachings of the Catholic religion, nor does it formulate all the duties of its members. Take, for instance, the matter of Sunday observance, attendance at divine service, and abstention from unnecessary servile work on that day. This is a matter upon which our Protestant neighbors have for many years laid great emphasis; yet nowhere in the Bible is the Sunday designated as the Lord's day; the day mentioned is the Sabbath, the last day of the week. The early Church, conscious of her authority to teach in the name of Christ, deliberately changed the day to Sunday: she did this to honor the day on which Christ rose from the dead and to signify that we are no longer under the Old Law of the Jews but under the New Law of Christ.

St. John ends his Gospel by telling us "there are also many other things which Jesus did which are not written in this book." St. Paul emphasizes the importance of holding fast to the teachings transmitted not only by writing but also by word of mouth: "Therefore, brethren, stand fast; and hold the traditions which you have learned, whether by word, or by our epistle" (2 Thessalonians 2:14). From all of which it must be abundantly clear that the Bible alone is not a safe and competent guide because it is not now and has never been accessible to all, because it is not clear and intelligible to all, and because it does not contain all the truths of the Christian religion.

MISUSE OF BIBLE

The folly of attempting to make the Bible alone serve as a guide for each individual in matters of doctrine is becoming recognized by an increasingly large number of Protestants. In the leading Protestant weekly, *The Christian Century*, this folly was pointed out by the editor, Rev. Charles Clayton Morrison. Writing on the "Protestant Misuse of the Bible," he declares: "Protestantism has put the Bible in the wrong place . . . It has put it in the place which Christianity accords to Jesus Christ alone."

Here is how they came to make so fatal a mistake. "The reformers," he continues, "reacting violently against the Roman Catholic system with the Pope as its head, were unwisely led to assume that it was necessary to set up an authority other than Christ Himself, which would unite Protestantism as Catholicism was united under the Papacy. The Bible, newly translated in the vernacular, and made available to the laity by the invention of printing, became this authority. It was to be the supreme tribunal of appeal."

Dr. Morrison points out that Luther had hardly begun his revolt when "the conference of Luther and Zwingli at Marburg, the intention of which was to unify the German and Swiss Reformations, broke down in an unhappy temper over the failure of the two leaders to agree on the interpretation of a single Biblical text: 'This is My Body.' From that day on the misuse of the Bible has vitiated the spirit of Protestantism, narrowed its vision, preoccupied it with petty contention, unendingly divided it into sects and warped the supreme character of the Bible itself."[2]

Thus at the very birth of Protestantism the poison of private judgment was injected into the offspring: a poison which has wrought such woeful dissension, strife and anarchy within its body ever since.

NEEDS LIVING INTERPRETER

That misuse has opened the door to the fatal misconception that each individual, regardless of education or lack of it, is able to interpret for himself all the books of the Bible: that fallacy has brought endless bickering and strife to Protestantism and has split it into myriads of warring sects and factions. We point this out not with glee but with sadness; we hope that the tragic error will be rectified so that the unity which prevailed before the religious upheaval of the 16th century may be restored to a distracted Christendom.

We have now shown the fallacy of the three claims put forth by well-meaning people to justify themselves in not becoming members

---

2. *The Christian Century*, June 5, 1946.

of Christ's Church. The fallacy of the contention that all religions are equally good and true, that sincerity is an adequate substitute for truth and for the effort to discover it, that the Bible alone is sufficient, has been uncovered so plainly and so unmistakably that even he who runs can see and understand. Having removed these misconceptions, we come now to the question of supreme practical importance: Which Is Christ's True Church? That is the question we answer in the following chapter.

Chapter 2

DIVINE ORIGIN OF CATHOLIC CHURCH

WHEN after careful consideration one comes to realize that it does matter what one believes, he finds himself confronted with the question: Which is Christ's true Church? The answer might be obtained by finding out which Church possesses the marks of *unity, sanctity, catholicity* and *apostolicity;* for these are the marks which Christ imprinted upon His Church to distinguish her from all others. It might prove somewhat tedious, however, to examine all of the several hundred Christian denominations to discover if any one of them possesses all these characteristics.

Besides, there is a shorter way of answering the query: Which is the true Church? This is by discovering: Which is the Church *founded* by Jesus Christ? For, if one can discover a Church founded directly and immediately by Christ and authorized to teach in His name, and to which He promised the abiding presence of the Spirit of Truth, then one can be certain that if the true Church is to be found anywhere on the earth, it must be that institution of which Christ Himself is the Founder.

CHRIST SPEAKS

Turn now to the pages of any reliable history, whether written by Jew, Protestant, Catholic or non-believer, and you will find that there is unanimous agreement among all historians that the Catholic Church at least was founded by Christ. The evidence of the Holy Scriptures, considered simply as historical documents, is too overwhelming to permit any doubt or quibbling on this point. Let us look at the solemn words whereby our divine Savior founded His Church and then clothed it with the power and authority to teach all mankind in His name.

The credentials are not confined to one Gospel, but are to be found in all four: the words are simple; their meaning is unmistakable. It is Christ Himself who is speaking to the Apostles: "As the

24

Father hath sent Me, I also send you" (John 20:21). "All power is given to Me in heaven and on earth. Going, therefore, teach ye all nations; baptizing them in the name of the Father, and of the Son, and of the Holy Ghost. Teaching them to observe all things whatsoever I have commanded you: and behold I am with you all days, even to the consummation of the world" (Matthew 28:18-20).

These words constitute the evidence of the Church's divinely appointed mission to teach the truths of Christ to all nations: they constitute the charter which the Church is to present to every generation as the imperishable credentials of her delegation as the duly accredited agency to teach in the name and with the authority of Jesus Christ. That the people hearing this divinely authorized teaching are not to regard themselves as free to accept or reject it, is made likewise clear by our divine Master: "Go ye into the whole world, and preach the gospel to every creature. He that believeth and is baptized, shall be saved: but he that believeth not shall be condemned" (Mark 16:15-16).

With equal clarity, St. Luke presents this same insistence of Christ on the duty of the faithful to accept the Gospel because of the authority which lies behind it: "He that heareth you, heareth Me, and he that despiseth you, despiseth Me; and he that despiseth Me, despiseth Him that sent Me" (Luke 10:16).

CHRIST COMMANDS HIS CHURCH TO TEACH

From these clear words of Christ, it is evident that our divine Savior did not follow the procedure imagined by many people today —the disinterested procedure of merely uttering certain religious and moral truths without establishing any institutions to interpret and to transmit them to future generations. The idea that Jesus simply enunciated certain truths and failed to provide any responsible agency for the transmission of these teachings to all mankind is not only uncomplimentary to the wisdom of Jesus and to His solicitude for the salvation of all mankind, but it also finds no warrant in Holy Scripture. To have placed upon each individual who was to be born into the world the task of ferreting out for himself from the mists of the historic past the precise teachings of Jesus, and the equally difficult task of interpreting them with unerring accuracy, would have been a procedure which would have foredoomed His enterprise to certain and inevitable failure.

Indeed, the overwhelming majority of mankind has neither the time nor the ability to accomplish so Herculean a task. It is to be remembered that not only was the printing press not then in existence, but that even the art of writing was the accomplishment of few. Furthermore, as has already been pointed out, there is no evidence that Christ ever wrote a line for a permanent record, or that He commanded any of His disciples to write.

On the contrary, His command to the Apostles was to preach, to teach, in season and out of season. This method renders it possible for the teacher to adapt the presentation of the Master's teachings to the varying capacities of his hearers to understand; it is the only effective method for the transmission of Christ's legacy of truth to mankind; it is the procedure, which the Scriptures disclose with unmistakable clearness, that Christ actually adopted. The impression so prevalent in non-Catholic circles, that Christ simply uttered certain truths 19 centuries ago, and then allows every individual to sink or swim in accordance with his ability to find out and to interpret for himself the precise meaning of His teachings, finds no support in the pages of Holy Writ.

THREE FUNDAMENTAL FACTS OF HISTORY

Hence it is most important that men and women nowadays be brought to realize three fundamental facts of history:

1. Jesus Christ actually founded a Church.

2. He conferred upon that Church the jurisdiction and the power to teach all mankind.

3. The Church which Christ founded and clothed with such power and authority is the Catholic Church.

From the above historical facts, there follows with inexorable logic the simple conclusion: The Catholic Church is the one true Church, established by Jesus Christ for the salvation of all mankind.

Is there any possible escape from this conclusion? While admitting, as all men must admit, that the Catholic Church was founded by Jesus Christ, some have sought to escape from the above conclusion by alleging that the Catholic Church in the course of ages ceased to teach the pure truths of Christ, introduced error, and therefore is not today to be regarded as the true Church.

But this can be true only if our Savior broke the promises He made to His Church when He said: "And behold I am with you all days, even to the consummation of the world," and "upon this rock I will build my Church and the gates of hell shall not prevail against it." If Christ broke those solemn promises, then we can confidently affirm that there is not today anywhere on the face of the earth the true Church of God.

That Christ did not break His pledge is evident from the fact that the Catholic Church is the only institution in Christendom which has come down through 1900 years teaching the world today the same deposit of divine truth which she taught to the Greeks and Romans, the Medes and the Persians in the first century.

CHRIST HAS FULFILLED HIS PROMISE

The Church has suffered from kings and emperors from the days of Nero to those of Communist terrorism and persecution in our own. In every land her children have suffered martyrdom for the faith; they have braved the executioner's sword; they have faced the wild lions in the Roman arena. They have withstood the burning fagots at the martyr's stake: neither have they quailed before the firing squads of the modern day.

The Church has witnessed the despoilation of her property by Henry VIII and the captivity of her supreme Pontiff by Napoleon Bonaparte. But she has not surrendered, either for king or peasant, one single bit of those divinely revealed truths which Jesus Christ commanded her to proclaim to all the nations of the world until the crack of doom.

She has withstood the acids of modern unbelief which have eaten so deeply into the traditional fabrics of other faiths; she has refused

27

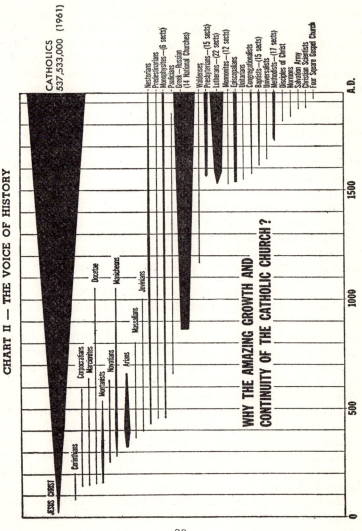

CHART II — THE VOICE OF HISTORY

WHY THE AMAZING GROWTH AND
CONTINUITY OF THE CATHOLIC CHURCH?

CATHOLICS
537,533,000 (1961)

JESUS CHRIST

Cerinthians
Carpocratians
Marcionites
Montanists
Novatians
Arians
Messalians
Docetae
Manicheans
Jovinians

Nestorians
Predestinarians
Monophysites—(6 sects)
Paulicians
Greek—Russian
(14 National Churches)
Waldenses
Presbyterians—(15 sects)
Lutherans—(22 sects)
Mennonites—(12 sects)
Episcopalians
Unitarians
Congregationalists
Baptists—(15 sects)
Universalists
Methodists—(17 sects)
Disciples of Christ
Mormons
Salvation Army
Christian Scientists
Four Square Gospel Church

A.D.

500   1000   1500

0

28

to surrender to the gilded paganism of the day, and has declined to lower her ethical standards to suit the demands of a pleasure loving world. She has refused to make compromise with Caesar by surrendering any of her sovereignty in the spiritual domain to the heightened nationalism and imperialism of the day. She preaches "Jesus Christ, yesterday, and today; and the same forever" (Hebrews 13:8). This perpetuity of the Church, this survival through all the ages, without the surrender of any of her truths, and without ever ceasing to carry her divine deposit of doctrine to all the nations of the world, is the blinding evidence that Christ has kept His promise to be with her all days. The Catholic Church today is as truly the Church of Christ as when she first came from the hands of her divine Founder 19 centuries ago in Judea.

THE VOICE OF HISTORY

Chart II, *The Voice of History,* shows at a glance that the Catholic Church is the only Church in the world today which traces her origin back to Christ. It shows that she alone was founded by Christ while all other Churches were established by men. It brings this into such clear relief that even he who runs may see that the Catholic Church with Christ for her Founder and Protector through all the centuries is the one true Church of Christ on earth.

The vertical lines indicate the centuries of the Christian era. The horizontal lines represent some of the larger and more important of the many hundreds of religious denominations that have risen during the past 19 centuries. Those lines indicate the duration of the various sects by beginning at the respective dates of origin, and ceasing when they disappeared. The width of the line shows the approximate size of the denomination.

It is to be noted that Protestantism first appears upon the earth in the 16th century, in contrast to the Catholic Church which had been in existence at that time for 1500 years, having been founded by Jesus Christ in Jerusalem in the year 33 A.D.

While the term "Protestantism" had its origin at the Diet of Spires in Germany in 1529, the first manifestation of the movement

CHART III — RECENT HUMAN ORIGINS AND DIVISIONS OF PROTESTANTISM AS SHOWN IN "LIFE" MAGAZINE

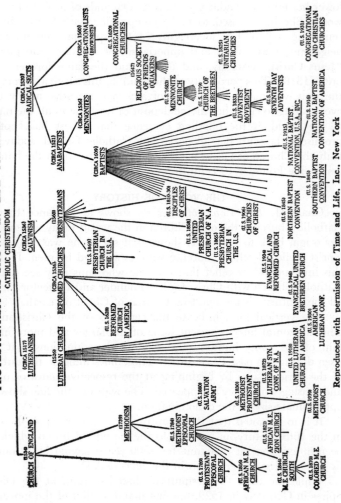

Reproduced with permission of Time and Life, Inc., New York

30

occurred when Martin Luther nailed his theses to the doors of the church at Wittenberg on October 31, 1517. All the other Protestant denominations were started by various human founders since that time. Contrast the divine origin of the Catholic Church with the human origins of all the Protestant Churches.

The comparatively recent origin of Protestant denominations is shown likewise in Chart III which was published in *Life* magazine. It also portrays the numerous divisions and the utter lack of unity within Protestantism. Note that the chart brings out that long before a single Protestant sect saw the light of day, the Catholic Church was carrying on her divinely appointed mission to mankind. Christendom, as the chart brings out, was Catholic: for Catholicity and historical Christianity are identical.

"TIME" SPEAKS OUT

This is the significant truth which *Time* magazine brought out in an article on the fragmentation of Protestantism as shown by the numerous sects composing the National Council of Churches and illustrated with a graph, aptly entitled, *Christian Chaos*. With chaos characterizing even the Council seeking to produce some semblance of unity, how, wonders *Time,* can anything but confusion result?

"Christendom (meaning 'all Christians collectively') is split," observes *Time,* "into disunited, sometimes warring, sects and churches, more than 250 in the U.S. alone. Protestants have lived with Christian fragmentation—and rationalized it with Christian double talk—for centuries (see Chart IV). But it has a way of bringing them up short whenever they confront the concept of 'The Church.' What is the Christian Church and where is it?"

Time continues: "Roman Catholics have a ready answer. The Church is the Church of Rome, and no other. Protestants cannot answer the question so easily. For them The Church can exist on this earth only as an ideal; its reality is in the future—and in heaven, where it is formed of 'the blessed company of all the faithful people.'

CHART IV

CHRISTIAN CHAOS (Simplified)

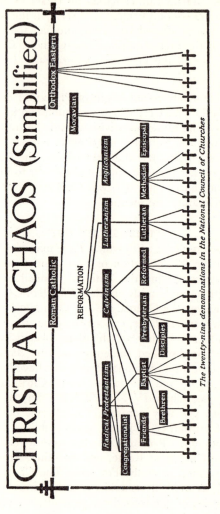

The twenty-nine denominations in the National Council of Churches

Time Chart by R. M. Chapin, Jr   Courtesy of *Time.*   Copyright *Time* Inc. 1951

But this is not a comfortable concept to many U.S. Protestants, who, as practical organization-minded men, would rather have the Church, like the Kingdom of Heaven, inhabit this earth.

"How," asks *Time*, "to bring that about? Again (if their tremendous premise is accepted), it is the Roman Catholics who have the simple, uncompromising, logical answer: unconditional surrender to Rome. Let all who call themselves Christians submit to the authority of the Roman Church, they say, and the unity of Christendom will thereby be established." The logic is inexorable, but the statement is unnecessarily harsh and oversimplified. The Catholic Church indeed hopes and prays for the "one fold" desired by Christ. But she expects it to be accomplished only in God's good time and she adapts her approach to the spirit of the times in which all good men long for a unity of which they know not the source.

Non-Catholics in increasing numbers, *Time* points out, are feeling this scandal of disunity.

"In the present century," *Time* says, "U. S. Protestants have been increasingly unhappy about themselves. Unhappiest of all were the missionaries, whose work spotlighted the absurdity of the Christian schism (How can you ask a Chinese in North China to become a Southern Baptist?)."

Heartsick at the sight of the 250 bickering sects of Protestantism destroying every vestige of that unity for which Christ pleaded so earnestly, the late Bishop Brent said: "In our hearts most of us are devotees of the cult of the incomplete—sectarianism. The Christ in one church often categorically denies the Christ in a neighboring church. It would be ludicrous were it not tragic." Yes, the only final solution to the problem of a divided Christendom is the unity of Christ. We should pray that this becomes ever more a reality in the see of Peter, the historic center of Christian unity, the Mother Church of all Christendom, where all will find a mother's love, the fullness of divine revelation, security, peace of mind and unity at last.

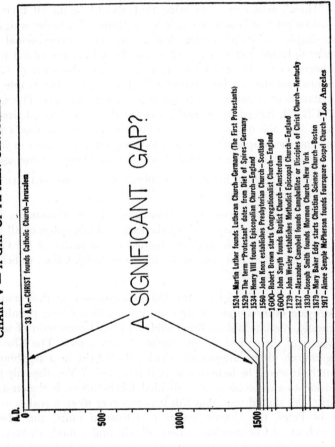

CHART V – A GAP OF FIFTEEN CENTURIES

A SIGNIFICANT GAP?

33 A.D.—CHRIST founds Catholic Church—Jerusalem

1524—Martin Luther founds Lutheran Church—Germany (The First Protestants)
1529—The term "Protestant" dates from Diet of Spires—Germany
1534—Henry VIII founds Episcopalian Church—England
1560—John Knox establishes Presbyterian Church—Scotland
1600—Robert Brown starts Congregationalist Church—England
1600—John Smyth founds Baptist Church—Amsterdam
1739—John Wesley establishes Methodist Episcopal Church—England
1827—Alexander Campbell founds Campbellites or Disciples of Christ Church—Kentucky
1830—Joseph Smith founds Mormon Church—New York
1879—Mary Baker Eddy starts Christian Science Church—Boston
1917—Aimee Semple McPherson founds Foursquare Gospel Church—Los Angeles

A.D.
0
500
1000
1500

Chart V, *A Gap of Fifteen Centuries,* focuses attention upon the *telltale gap* of 15 centuries that yawns between the foundation of Christ's Church in 33 to the establishment of Lutheranism, the first form of Protestantism, in 1524. Why is that gap significant? Because it brings out so clearly and so simply the fact that a Church which did not see the light of day for 15 or more centuries after Christ had ascended into heaven, cannot simply claim to be the Church Christ promised to be with forever.

These charts bring out more clearly and more vividly than a volume of a thousand pages the following important historical facts.

1. The Catholic Church alone has Jesus Christ for her Founder.

2. She had been carrying on her divinely appointed work of teaching the religion of Christ to mankind for 15 centuries before Protestantism began.

3. The various forms of Protestantism are without full divine sanction or approval.

4. Loyalty to Christ demands that one do all in his power to cooperate with God's grace and embrace the religion founded by Jesus Christ for all mankind.

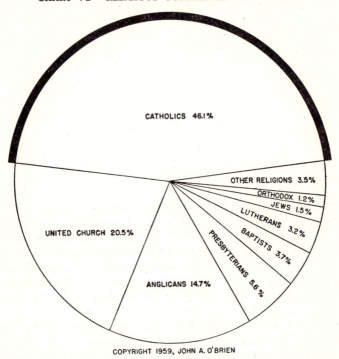

Chart Va, *Religious Complexion of Canada,* brings out strikingly the fact that Catholics constitute 46.1%, or almost one-half of the church affiliated population of Canada.

It is another evidence of the tremendous vitality of the Catholic religion as well as the fulfillment of Christ's promise to be with His Church always.

Table I, *The Title Deed of the Catholic Church,* shows the unbroken list of pontiffs from St. Peter to today. That is the evidence of history that the Catholic Church speaks to the world today with the authority of Jesus Christ. Why? Because Christ constituted Peter the visible head of His Church on earth and clothed his office with supreme and infallible teaching authority. We know that our present pontiff speaks to us with the same authority because his title goes back in unbroken succession to Peter and through Peter to Christ.

If you were about to purchase a piece of property, would you not examine the title deed to make sure that it goes back all the way to the original owner? If it did not, you would know that the title is worthless. Why not exercise the same care in your search for the true Church of Jesus Christ? If you examine the title deeds of all the Churches calling themselves Christian, you will find that only one goes back to Peter and to Christ—the Holy, Catholic, Apostolic Church, founded by Christ and governed by Peter and his successors in an unbroken line down to the present day.

Table I

THE SUPREME ROMAN PONTIFFS

St. Peter of Bethsaida in Galilee, Prince of the Apostles, who received from Jesus Christ the Supreme Pontifical Power to be transmitted to his Successors, resided first at Antioch, then at Rome for twenty-five years where he was martyred in the year 64, or 67 of the common reckoning.

END OF PONTIFICATE,	A.D.	END OF PONTIFICATE,	A.D.
St. Linus, M.	76	St. Anterus, M.	236
St. Anacletus or Cletus, M.	88	St. Fabian, M.	250
St. Clement I, M,	97	St. Cornelius, M.	253
St. Evaristus, M.	105	St. Lucius I, M.	254
St. Alexander I, M.	115	St. Stephen I, M.	257
St. Sixtus I, M.	125	St. Sixtus II, M.	258
St. Telesphorus, M.	136	St. Dionysius	268
St. Hyginus, M.	140	St. Felix I, M.	274
St. Pius I, M.	155	St. Eutychian, M.	283
St. Anicetus, M.	166	St. Caius, M.	296
St. Soterus, M.	175	St. Marcellinus, M.	304
St. Eleuterius, M.	189	St. Marcellus I, M.	309
St. Victor I, M.	199	St. Eusebius, M.	309
St. Zephyrinus, M.	217	St. Melchiades, M.	314
St. Callistus I, M.	222	St. Sylvester, I	335
St. Urban I, M.	230	St. Mark	336
St. Pontain, M.	235	St. Julius I	352

END OF PONTIFICATE,	A.D.	END OF PONTIFICATE,	A.D.
Liberius	366	Sisinnius	708
St. Damasus I	384	Constantine	715
St. Siricius	399	St. Gregory II	731
St. Anastasius I	401	St. Gregory III	741
St. Innocent I	417	St. Zachary	752
St. Zozimus	418	Stephen III	757
St. Boniface I	422	St. Paul I	767
St. Celestine I	432	Stephen IV	772
St. Sixtus III	440	Adrian I	795
St. Leo I (the Great)	461	St. Leo III	816
St. Hilary	468	Stephen V	817
St. Simplicius	483	St. Paschal I	824
St. Felix III or II	492	Eugene II	827
St. Gelasius I	496	Valentine	827
Anastasius II	498	Gregory IV	844
St. Symmacus	514	Sergius II	847
St. Hormisdas	523	St. Leo IV	855
St. John I	526	Benedict III	858
St. Felix IV or III	530	St. Nicholas I (the Great)	867
Boniface II	532	Adrian II	872
John II	535	John VIII	882
St. Agapitus	536	Marinus I	884
St. Silverius, M.	537	St. Adrian III	885
Vigilius	555	Stephen VI	891
Pelagius I	561	Formosus	896
John III	574	Boniface VI	896
Benedict I	579	Stephen VII	897
Pelagius II	590	Romanus	897
St. Gregory I (the Great)	604	Theodore II	897
Sabinianus	606	John IX	900
Boniface III	607	Benedict IV	903
St. Boniface IV	615	Leo V	903
St. Deusdeditus or Adeodatus I	618	Sergius III	911
Boniface V	625	Anastasius III	913
Honorius I	638	Landus	914
Severinus	640	John X	928
John IV	642	Leo VI	928
Theodore I	649	Stephen VIII	931
St. Martin I, M.	655	John XI	935
St. Eugene I	657	Leo VII	939
St. Vitalian	672	Stephen IX	942
Adeodatus II	676	Marinus II	946
Donus I	678	Agapitus II	955
St. Agathonus	681	John XII	964
St. Leo II	683	Leo VIII	965
St. Benedict II	685	Benedict V	966
John V	686	John XIII	972
Conon	687	Benedict VI	974
St. Sergius I	701	Benedict VII	983
John VI	705	John XIV	984
John VII	707	John XV	996

END OF PONTIFICATE,	A.D.	END OF PONTIFICATE,	A.D.
Gregory V	999	Martin IV	1285
Sylvester II	1003	Honorius IV	1287
John XVII	1003	Nicholas IV	1292
John XVIII	1009	St. Celestine V	1296
Sergius IV	1012	Boniface VIII	1303
Benedict VIII	1024	B. Benedict XI	1304
John XIX	1032	Clement V	1314
Benedict IX	1044	John XXII	1334
Benedict IX	1045	Benedict XII	1342
Sylvester III	1045	Clement VI	1352
Gregory VI	1046	Innocent VI	1362
Clement II	1047	B. Urban V	1370
Benedict IX	1048	Gregory XI	1378
Damasus II	1048	Urban VI	1389
St. Leo IX	1054	Boniface IX	1404
Victor II	1057	Innocent VII	1406
Stephen X	1058	Gregory XII	1415
Nicholas II	1061	Martin V	1431
Alexander II	1073	Eugene IV	1447
St. Gregory VII	1085	Nicholas V	1455
B. Victor VIII	1087	Callistus III	1458
B. Urban II	1099	Pius II	1464
Paschal II	1118	Paul II	1471
Gelasius II	1119	Sixtus IV	1484
Callistus II	1124	Innocent VIII	1492
Honorius II	1130	Alexander VI	1503
Innocent II	1143	Pius III	1503
Celestine II	1144	Julius II	1513
Lucius II	1145	Leo X	1521
B. Eugene III	1153	Adrian VI	1523
Anastasius IV	1154	Clement VII	1534
Adrian IV	1159	Paul III	1549
Alexander III	1181	Julius III	1555
Lucius III	1185	Marcellus II	1555
Urban III	1187	Paul IV	1559
Gregory VIII	1187	Pius IV	1565
Clement III	1191	St. Pius V	1572
Celestine III	1198	Gregory XIII	1585
Innocent III	1216	Sixtus V	1590
Honorius III	1227	Urban VII	1590
Gregory IX	1241	Gregory XIV	1591
Celestine IV	1241	Innocent IX	1591
Innocent IV	1254	Clement VIII	1605
Alexander IV	1261	Leo XI	1605
Urban IV	1264	Paul V	1621
Clement IV	1268	Gregory XV	1623
B. Gregory X	1276	Urban VIII	1644
B. Innocent V	1276	Innocent X	1655
Adrian V	1276	Alexander VII	1667
John XXI	1277	Clement IX	1669
Nicholas III	1280	Clement X	1676

END OF PONTIFICATE,	A.D.
Innocent XI	1689
Alexander VIII	1691
Innocent XII	1700
Clement XI	1721
Innocent XIII	1724
Benedict XIII	1730
Clement XII	1740
Benedict XIV	1758
Clement XIII	1769
Clement XIV	1774
Pius VI	1799
Pius VII	1823

END OF PONTIFICATE,	A.D.
Leo XII	1829
Pius VIII	1830
Gregory XVI	1846
Pius IX	1878
Leo XIII	1903
St. Pius X	1914
Benedict XV	1922
Pius XI	1939
Pius XII	1958
John XXIII	1963
Paul VI	

Chapter 3

CATHOLIC CHURCH ALONE IS APOSTOLIC

CONFIRMATION of the all important fact that the Catholic Church alone was founded by Christ and governed by His divinely appointed vicars on earth is proved not only by her unbroken list of pontiffs—the unassailable title deed of her divine origin—but also by the fact that she alone has retained *all* the teachings of Christ. Her doctrinal code today is that of the Apostolic Church of the first century. This identity of doctrine and of practice places upon the Church's title deed the telltale fingerprints of Christ and the Apostles.

Those fingerprints show that her doctrines are not the work of human teachers. They stamp the Church with the seal of divine origin and divine authorization.

Many doctrines of the Apostolic Church are no longer found in the creeds of our separated brethren. We shall cite in parallel columns a few of the basic teachings of Christ and the Apostles showing the identity of such doctrines with the Catholic faith, and the departure from those truths by Protestant denominations.

APOSTOLIC CHURCH	CATHOLIC CHURCH THE HOLY EUCHARIST	PROTESTANT CHURCHES
Jesus and the Apostles taught that the Holy Eucharist contains the Body and Blood of Christ: "Take ye, and eat. This is my body . . . drink ye all of this, for this is my blood . . ." (Matthew 26:26-28). "The chalice of benediction, which we bless, is it not the communion of the blood of Christ? And the bread, which we break, is it not the partaking of the body of the Lord?" (I Corinthians 10:16).	The Catholic Church holds fast to the clear teaching of Christ and the Apostles that the Holy Eucharist contains the Body and Blood of Jesus under the appearance of bread and wine.	Protestant Churches, with the exception of branches of the Episcopal and Lutheran churches, reject the doctrine of the Real Presence as idolatrous. They regard the partaking of communion as the receiving of a mere memorial or symbol of Christ's Body.

APOSTOLIC CHURCH	CATHOLIC CHURCH	PROTESTANT CHURCHES

POWER OF PARDONING

Christ conferred upon the Apostles the power to forgive sins: "Whose sins you shall forgive, they are forgiven them" (John 20-23). St. Paul mirrors the faith of the Apostolic Church when he writes: "God hath given to us the ministry of reconciliation" (II Corinthians 5:18).	As the inheritors of the power and authority of the Apostles, the bishops and priests of the Catholic Church exercise the ministry of reconciliation, forgiving penitent sinners in the name of Jesus Christ.	Protestant Churches reject the sacrament of Confession and deny that God delegated to man the power of pardoning sinners in His name.

EXTREME UNCTION

Mirroring the faith of the Apostolic Church, St. James says: "Is any man sick among you? Let him bring in the priests of the Church, and let them pray over him anointing him with oil in the name of the Lord" (James 5:14).	In conformity with the injunction of St. James, priests of the Catholic Church pray over the sick and anoint them with oil in the name of the Lord, thus administering the ancient sacrament of Extreme Unction.	Few Protestant Churches observe the practice of anointing the sick, notwithstanding the clear injunction of the Apostle.

MARRIAGE BOND UNBREAKABLE

Christ taught that the bond of Christian marriage is unbreakable and forbade divorce, saying: "What therefore God hath joined together let no man put asunder" (Matthew 19:6). "Whosoever shall put away his wife and marry another, committeth adultery against her. And if the wife shall put away her husband, and be married to another, she committeth adultery" (Mark 10:11-12).	In compliance with Christ's command, the Catholic Church proclaims the indissoluble character of Christian marriage and forbids divorce.	Protestant denominations have departed from Christ's teaching and some of them remarry persons who have been divorced for the most trivial reasons.

CONFIRMATION

The Apostles, Peter and John, confirmed the newly baptized in Samaria. They "Prayed for them, that they might receive the Holy Ghost. For he was not as yet come upon any of them; but they were only baptized in the name of the Lord Jesus. Then they laid their hands upon them, and they received the Holy Ghost" (Acts 8:15-17).	As a successor of the Apostles, every Catholic bishop likewise prays over baptized persons and imposes hands upon them in the sacrament of Confirmation through which they receive the Holy Ghost.	With the exception of Episcopalians, Methodists and some Lutherans—and even they do not recognize it as a sacrament—no Protestant Church in this country imposes hands upon the baptized.

APOSTOLIC CHURCH	CATHOLIC CHURCH PRIMACY OF PETER	PROTESTANT CHURCHES
Christ made Peter the head of the Apostles and conferred upon him the power of ruling His Church: "Thou art Peter; and upon this rock I will build my Church . . . I will give to thee the keys of the kingdom of heaven" (Matthew 16:18-19). "Confirm thy brethren" (Luke 22:32). "Feed my lambs . . . Feed my sheep" (John 21:16-17).	In conformity with Our Savior's teaching, the Catholic Church gives the primacy of honor and of jurisdiction to Peter and to his successors.	Protestant Churches practically deny the supremacy of Peter over the other Apostles and do not acknowledge the authority of his successors.

INFALLIBLE TEACHING AUTHORITY

Christ conferred upon Peter and the other Apostles the power of teaching His doctrines with inerrancy. The Apostles exercised this power, and the Apostolic Church recognized and perpetuated it. "When you have received of us the word of the hearing of God, you received it not as the word of men, but (as it is indeed) the word of God" (Thessalonians 2:13). "It hath seemed good to the Holy Ghost and to us," say the assembled Apostles, "to lay no further burden upon you than these necessary things" (Acts 15:28). "Though we, or an angel from heaven, preach a gospel to you besides that which we have preached to you, let him be anathema" (Galatians 1:8).	Perpetuating the faith of the Apostolic Church, the Catholic Church alone proclaims the teachings of Christ with infallible authority. United with the Holy See, her ministers preach with authority, and the faithful receive with implicit confidence what the Church teaches, because of the promise of Christ to be with her "all days," protecting her from error and falsehood.	No Protestant Church teaches with infallible authority or even claims to possess it. Protestant ministers proclaim no authoritative doctrines but advance their opinions, reflecting their own interpretation of the Bible. Their listeners claim the same right as their ministers to interpret the Scriptures according to their own private judgment. Hence the confusion and ceaseless differences among them.

Christ conferred upon His Church the power and authority not only to teach His doctrines but also to administer His sacraments. These are the channels through which the fruits of the Redemption are applied to the individual soul; they are thus channels of divine grace. Each sacrament was constituted by Christ for a particular purpose and each sacrament imparts a grace which helps to achieve

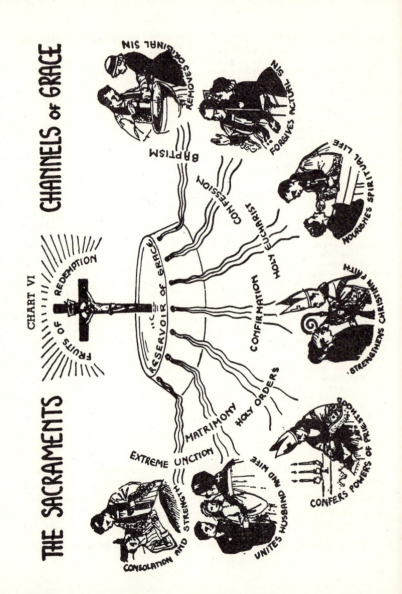

the end for which it was instituted; this grace is called sacramental grace. Chart VI shows how the graces and fruits of the Redemption are applied through each of the seven sacraments to the soul of the individual.

CEASELESS DIVISION WITHIN PROTESTANTISM

In contrast with the unbroken continuity of the Catholic Church through 1900 years, preserving her unity of faith inviolate under one supreme spiritual head, are the various sects which arose in the course of the centuries and which are conspicuous for the lateness of their arrival upon the stage of Christendom, for their impermanence and instability, and for the divisions and disintegrations which have gone steadily on within their own ranks. The heretical sects which sprang up in the early centuries, such as the Novatians, Macedonians and Pelagians, have disappeared from the earth, leaving only their names and the memory of their errors to posterity. As the branch of the tree cut from the trunk is deprived of life-giving sap, and thus speedily withers and dies, so these sects, when separated from the Mother Church, were deprived of the life-giving graces flowing through her sacramental veins to all the members of her organic body and speedily withered and died.

It was the realization of this truth that brought the gifted scholar, John Henry Newman of Oxford University, England, into the fold of Christ. While engaged in his great historical investigation of the Monophysites and other heretical sects in early ages, the startling question suddenly burst upon him: "Am I not after all in the same relative position to the Church of Christ as the Monophysites of the fifth century?" As he surveyed the innumerable divisions within Protestantism, the query persisted: "What is the difference in the position of all the Protestant sects who cut themselves off from the historic centre of unity in the 16th century and the heretical sects which did the same in the fifth?" The question gripped him and would not let him rest.

In his classic *Apologia Pro Vita Sua* he describes his sudden realization of the analogous position of Protestants of the 16th century and of his own day to the heretical sects of the fifth century. "There was an awful similitude," he writes, "more awful, because so silent and unimpassioned, between the dead records of the past and the feverish chronicle of the present. . . . My stronghold was antiquity; now here, in the middle of the fifth century, I found as it seemed to me, Christendom of the 16th and 19th centuries reflected. I saw my face in the mirror," he adds with horror, "and I was a Monophysite."

CARDINAL NEWMAN'S SURRENDER TO TRUTH

The penetrating realization of the implications of that historical analogy that now loomed up vividly before him, stubborn and ineradicable, proved to be the turning point in his life. It was not without a terrific struggle that he surrendered. With all the might of his powerful intellect he struggled valiantly to establish some logical justification for Anglicanism as a sect or "branch" distinct from Rome. But all his continued research into the records of history served only to convince him beyond all possibility of doubts that the Catholic Church alone was founded by Christ, and that she alone retained in their fullness the teachings of the Apostles. The conclusion which follows with irresistible logic, that the Catholic Church is the one true Church of Christ on earth, brought this gifted scholar, as it has brought many other brilliant minds both before and since his day, into the fold of Christ.

In the 20th century, as surely as in the fifth, when a branch is torn from the trunk of a tree it withers and dies. The constant divisions and ceaseless disintegration which have been taking place within Protestantism since it separated from the Mother Church are after all but forms of institutional withering and creedal death. Not a single one of the founders of a Protestant creed, if he returned to earth today, would recognize either his creed or his progeny.

Table II presents the date, place of origin and the names of the founders of the leading Protestant denominations as recorded by non-Catholic authorities, chiefly the United States Religious Census. Study that table carefully. It shows that the first form of Protestantism did not see the light of day until the 16th century—1500 years after Christ had founded the Catholic Church. In 1524, Martin Luther established the Lutheran Church; ten years later, Henry VIII set up the Anglican Church in England; Amsterdam witnessed the founding of the Baptist Church by John Smyth in 1600; John and Charles Wesley established the Methodist Episcopal Church in England in 1739. All these denominations claim human founders; all of them rejected one or more of the fundamental doctrines of historic Christianity and introduced new tenets.

Table II
DATE, PLACE OF ORIGIN, FOUNDERS OF VARIOUS CHURCHES

Name	Year	Founders	Origin	Authority
Catholic	33	Jesus Christ	Jerusalem	New Testament
Lutheran	1524	Martin Luther	Germany	S. S. Schmucker in *History of All Denominations*
Episcopalian	1534	Henry VIII	England	Macaulay and other English Historians
Presbyterian	1560	John Knox	Scotland	Religious Bodies: 1936 U.S. Religious Census
Baptist	1600	John Smyth	Amsterdam	,,
Congregational	1600	Robert Brown	England	,,
Methodist Episcopal	1739	John and Charles Wesley	England	,,
United Brethren	1800	Philip Otterbein and Martin Boehm	Maryland	,,
Disciples of Christ	1827	Thomas and Alexander Campbell	Kentucky	,,
Mormon	1830	Joseph Smith	New York	,,
Salvation Army	1865	William Booth	London	,,
Christian Science	1879	Mary Baker Eddy	Boston	,,
Four-Square Gospel	1917	Aimee Semple McPherson	Los Angeles	,,

WHOM SHALL WE BELIEVE?

Whom shall the earnest searcher after truth believe—Martin Luther, Henry VIII, John Smyth, John Wesley, or their followers? There is reason and surety in the conclusion that the Church which Jesus Christ founded is to be accepted by all men as the one and only true Church of Christ on earth.

The speed with which the dissenting denominations split and

disintegrated among themselves is evident from the fact that in America today there are more than 300 denominations, all disagreeing with one another. Indeed, the larger denominations have undergone a ceaseless division within their own groups. Thus the last U. S. Religious Census reports no fewer than 20 different divisions within the Lutheran denomination, no fewer than 17 within the Methodist and 10 within the Presbyterian denomination. Within the Baptist Church there are 21 different divisions—grim evidence of the internal dissension that has been ceaselessly at work within the bosom of Protestantism.

Among the divisions listed in the Baptist Church are: Northern Baptist Convention, Southern Baptist Convention, Negro Baptists, American Baptist Association, Christian Unity Baptist Association, Colored Primitive Baptists, Duck River and Kindred Associations of Baptists (Baptists Church of Christ), Free Will Baptists, General Baptists, General Six Principle Baptists, Independent Baptist Church of America, National Baptist Evangelical Life and Soul Saving, National Assembly of the United States of America; Primitive Baptists, Regular Baptists, General Association of Regular Baptist Churches in the United States of America, Separate Baptists, Seventh Day Baptists, Seventh Day Baptists (German 1728), Two-Seed-in-the-Spirit Predestinarian Baptists, United American Free Will Baptist Church (Colored), United Baptists.

Bewildering as is this multitudinous splitting within the Baptist denomination, it does not, however, tell the whole story. There are branches and offshoots from this denomination, as there are from other denominations, wherein the name of the original Church has been sloughed off and in consequence they are no longer listed as divisions of the same. This fact is illustrated in the listing of the U. S. Religious Census of the various religious denominations. Thus immediately following the list of the previously enumerated divisions of the Baptist denomination, there is listed the following: "Brethren, German Baptist (dunkers)." Herein it is evident that the German Baptist Body, commonly known as Dunkers, is officially listed as

Brethren, though it has actually stemmed from the Baptist parent trunk. This instance of fission or splitting, with the loss of the parent name, has occurred times without number in the major Protestant denominations.

IS THIS "ONE FOLD"?

Is this the "one fold" and the "one faith" in which Jesus wished all His followers to be united and for which He prayed so fervently shortly before His death upon Calvary's Cross?

No; on the contrary, it is the confirmation which the 20th century offers of the persistence of that spirit of internal strife and dissension which characterized the activities of the Reformers in the 16th century. That this spirit alarmed even the Reformers themselves is evident from the following passage in a letter Calvin wrote to Melanchthon:

"It is of great importance that the divisions which subsist among us should not be known to future ages; for nothing can be more ridiculous than that we who have been compelled to make a separation from the whole world, should have agreed so ill among ourselves from the beginning of the Reformation."[1] It is the persistence of this spirit of internal discord and dissension which split Protestantism into so many hundred warring sects that recently caused the Rev. Peter Ainslie, a Disciple of Christ minister at Baltimore, to characterize this multiplicity of sects as "the scandal of Christendom."

---

1. *Epist.* 141.

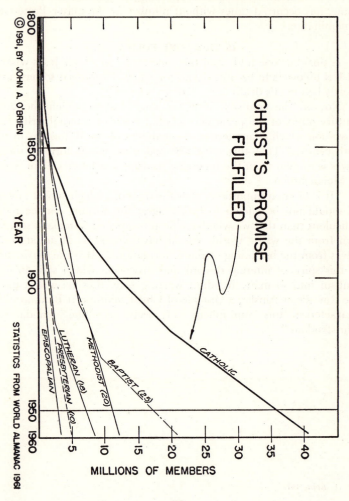

CHART VII — GROWTH OF CHURCHES IN U.S.A.

© 1961, BY JOHN A. O'BRIEN

CHRIST'S PROMISE
FULFILLED

YEAR

1800

1850

1900

1950
1960

STATISTICS FROM WORLD ALMANAC 1961

CATHOLIC

BAPTIST (2.5)

METHODIST (2.0)

PRESBYTERIAN (1.0)

LUTHERAN (1.5)

EPISCOPALIAN

MILLIONS OF MEMBERS

5   10   15   20   25   30   35   40

50

CHRIST FULFILLS HIS PROMISE

Chart VII, *The Growth of Churches in the U.S.A.,* shows how the Catholic Church has outstripped all in the marvelous rapidity of her climb to her present position of numerical superiority. In 1785 there were but about 23,000 white Catholics ministered to by 34 priests, according to Bishop Carroll, the Prefect Apostolic. They thus constituted considerably less than one per cent of the population.

From a little colony of immigrants they have increased by leaps and bounds, until today they constitute by far the largest religious body in the United States. Their rapid rise to numerical ascendancy in spite of discrimination, opposition and slander, offers a striking parallel to the marvelous growth of the early Christians from an impoverished and persecuted minority to the dominant religious organization in the Grecian and Roman empires.

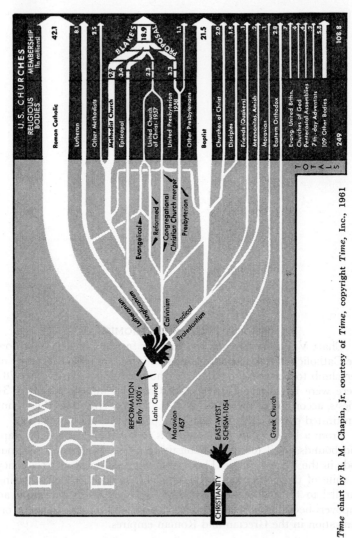

FLOW OF FAITH

U.S. CHURCHES

RELIGIOUS BODIES

MEMBERSHIP (in millions)

Religious Bodies	Membership
Roman Catholic	42.1
Lutheran	8.1
Other Methodists	2.5
Methodist Church	18.9
Episcopal	3.4
United Church of Christ–1957	2.3
United Presbyterian–1958	
Other Presbyterians	1.1
Baptist	21.5
Churches of Christ	2.0
Disciples	1.8
Friends (Quakers)	.1
Mennonites, Amish	.1
Moravian	2.9
Eastern Orthodox	.7
Evang. United Breth.	.7
Churches of God	.4
Pentecostal Assemblies	.3
7th-day Adventists	5.8
109 Other Bodies	

TOTALS 249 — 108.8

BLAKE's PROPOSAL 12.9

Evangelical
Reformed
Congregational
Christian Church merger
Presbyterian

Lutheranism
Anglicanism
Calvinism
Radical Protestantism

REFORMATION Early 1500's

Latin Church
Moravian 1457

EAST–WEST SCHISM–1054

Greek Church

CHRISTIANITY

Time chart by R. M. Chapin, Jr. courtesy of *Time*, copyright *Time*, Inc., 1961

52

VITALITY OF THE CHURCH

The apostolicity, unity and vitality of the Catholic Church are mirrored in Chart VIII, *The Flow of Faith,* prepared by *Time* magazine to show the merger of four denominations, proposed by Dr. E. C. Blake.

Recognizing that the disunity of Protestantism with its more than 250 divisions is directly contrary to Christ's teaching concerning the unity that is the distinctive mark of the true fold, Dr. Blake, Stated Clerk of the Presbyterian General Assembly, proposed the merger of the Methodist, Episcopal, United Church of Christ and United Presbyterian. The chart brings out strikingly the antiquity of the Catholic religion, the historical Christianity established by Christ, which has flowed unbrokenly from the time of our Lord down to the present day. In contrast, all the Protestant sects have sprung from the Reformation in the sixteenth century.

The chart depicts also the vitality of the Catholic Church which has a membership of 42.1 million (1960 census) in the U.S.A., dwarfing all the Protestant denominations. The largest of these is the Baptist Church, but in its total membership are lumped together all the 21 different divisions or sects of Baptists. In contrast with such diversity of creed, all the members of the Catholic Church profess the same faith and acknowledge the same supreme spiritual head, the pope, the successor of St. Peter.

"Disunity in the name of Christ," comments *Time,* "is a scandal and a shame." Pointing out how easily Protestants switch from one denomination to another, *Time* continues: "If U.S. Protestants think of themselves as Presbyterians or Methodists, they tend more and more to pick their churches because they are within walking distance, or because their friends go there, or because they like the preacher—all too few care passionately about doctrinal differences between the limestone church with stained glass, the spired white clapboard and the Georgian brick. Typical is a Hollywood man whose parents were Lutherans and then Methodists; he became a Presbyterian 'because the bass soloist's position was open.' "

Time thinks that one element in the "homogenization of U.S.

Protestantism is the decline of ethnic differences between Americans; many a church used to be kept alive by the national loyalties of first-generation citizens and the parental loyalties of their children. Another element is the pressure on Protestantism of an expanding Roman Catholic Church, which is currently growing *more than twice as fast* as the leading Protestant denominations."

Dismayed at the appalling disunity of Protestantism's 250 divisions in the U.S.A. alone, Dr. Blake said: "I don't believe it is God's

CHART IX — THE RELIGIOUS COMPLEXION OF THE UNITED STATES

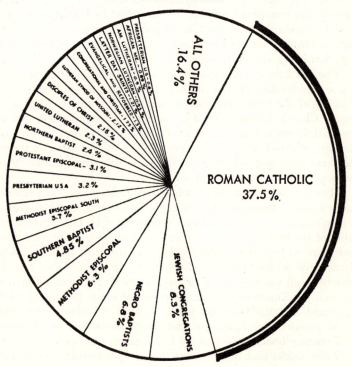

ALL OTHERS
16.4%

PRESBYTERIAN U.S. 0.8%
AFRICAN ME. 0.85%
AM. LUTHERAN 0.9%
NORWEGIAN LUTHERAN 0.95%
EVANGELICAL AND CHRISTIAN 1.13%
LATTER DAY SAINTS 1.2%
CONGREGATIONAL AND REFORMED 1.75%
LUTHERAN SYNOD OF MISSOURI 2.12%
DISCIPLES OF CHRIST 2.15%
UNITED LUTHERAN 2.3%
NORTHERN BAPTIST 2.4%
PROTESTANT EPISCOPAL – 3.1%
PRESBYTERIAN USA 3.2%
METHODIST EPISCOPAL SOUTH 3.7%
SOUTHERN BAPTIST 4.85%
METHODIST EPISCOPAL 6.3%
NEGRO BAPTISTS 6.8%
JEWISH CONGREGATIONS 8.3%

ROMAN CATHOLIC
37.5%

will to have so many churches in the United States." How right he is! Christ founded but one Church, one fold, one faith, and He wants all to be members thereof. Jesus prayed "that all may be one, even as thou, Father, in me and I in thee; that they also may be one in us, that the world may believe that thou hast sent me" (John 17:21).

Chart IX, *The Religious Complexion of the United States* (1936), is taken from the U.S. Federal Census and bears additional witness to the fact that the Catholic Church towers head and shoulders above every other religious organization in our country. Both these charts offer abundant evidence that Jesus Christ is keeping the promise which He made to the Church in the first century: "And behold I am with you *all* days, even to the consummation of the world" (Matthew 28:20).

The beloved disciple of Christ, St. John, placed his discerning finger upon the salient reason why the Catholic Church has withstood the fall of empires and the invasion of the barbarians which caused even the mighty empire of Rome to collapse; why she has withstood the religious upheaval of the 16th century which shook Christendom to its very foundation, and why she is able to withstand today the acids of modern unbelief and the enervating influence of a gilded paganism, when back in the first century he exclaimed with prophetic foresight: "For whatsoever is *born of God,* overcometh the world: and this is the victory which overcometh the world, our faith" (I John 5:4). Because the Catholic Church was founded directly and immediately by Jesus Christ, because He has remained with her through the ages, protecting her from error, the Church remains today as she has been throughout the past 1900 years, the one true Church of Jesus Christ on earth.

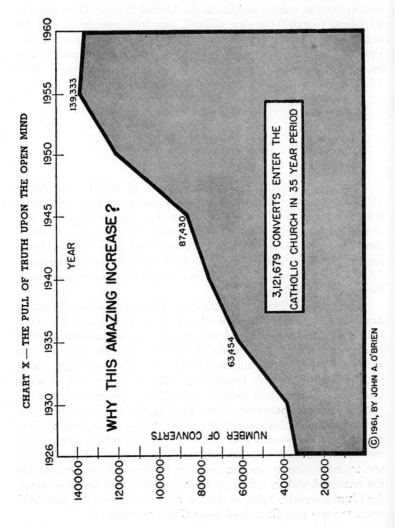

CHART X — THE PULL OF TRUTH UPON THE OPEN MIND

WHY THIS AMAZING INCREASE?

3,121,679 CONVERTS ENTER THE CATHOLIC CHURCH IN 35 YEAR PERIOD

NUMBER OF CONVERTS

YEAR

1926 1930 1935 1940 1945 1950 1955 1960

63,454   87,430   139,333

© 1961, BY JOHN A. O'BRIEN

Chart X, *The Pull of Truth Upon the Open Mind,* shows the constantly increasing numbers of converts to the Catholic Church in the United States. In 1926 converts totalled 35,751; in 1934 they totalled 63,454; in 1955 they reached the total of 139,333—making a grand total for the 35-year period of 3,121,679.

Many of the most brilliant minds in America have thought themselves into the Catholic Church. That line we trace from Orestes A. Brownson, a profound philosopher, to Bishop Frederick J. Kinsman, one of the most scholarly of all Anglican divines, down to Professor Carlton J. Hayes, the outstanding historian of Columbia University. The reasons which brought this galaxy of brilliant scholars, as well as the other 3,121,679 converts into the Church, can all, as G. K. Chesterton pointed out, be reduced to the one reason: *Catholicism is true.*

"The other day," wrote Professor William Lyon Phelps, "I read as a piece of news that in 50 years science will have destroyed religion, so that there will be nothing left of it except a memory. Meanwhile conversions to the Roman Catholic Church continue in such quantity and quality as to excite the attention of all who are interested in what is called the trend of modern thought. I recommend to those who wonder 'how any intelligent man can become a Roman Catholic' a little book called *Restoration,* written by Ross J. S. Hoffman, a professor of history in New York University, who tells us how he went from nothing to everything."

The noted author, John L. Stoddard, thus summarizes what his conversion has brought to him: "The Catholic Church has given me order for confusion, certainty for doubt, sunlight for darkness, substance for shadow." Therein is reflected the experience of all converts.

Chapter 4

CHRIST'S PLAN FOR HIS CHURCH

AS SKETCHED IN THE BIBLE

JESUS CHRIST founded the Catholic Church and stamped it with the marks by which it can easily be distinguished from the sects and creeds started by men. He is the Architect who specified not only the general structure of His Church but also its various parts. The blueprint of Christ's plan for His Church is contained in the Bible. Since all Christians recognize the authority of the inspired word of God, it will be well to present in some detail Christ's plan for His Church as outlined in Holy Scripture. This is done in the following sketch.

CHRIST FOUNDS HIS CHURCH

Christ Jesus Christ founds His Church in Jerusalem, A.D. 33, and commissions the Apostles to spread His teachings to all nations, saying to them:

"All power is given to Me in heaven and in earth. Going therefore, teach ye all nations; baptizing them in the name of the Father, and of the Son, and of the Holy Ghost. Teaching them to observe all things whatsoever I have commanded you: and behold I am with you all days, even to the consummation of the world" (Matthew 28:18-20).

Appearing to the Apostles in the upper chamber after His resurrection, Christ thus addressed them:

"As the Father hath sent Me, I also send you" (John 20:21).

CHRIST APPOINTS PETER

Peter Christ chooses Peter to be chief of the Apostles and the visible head of His Church on earth, saying to him:

"Thou art Peter; and upon this rock I will build my church, and the gates of hell shall not prevail against it. And I will give to thee the keys of the kingdom of heaven. And whatsoever thou shalt bind upon earth, it shall be bound also in heaven; and whatsoever thou shalt loose on earth, it shall be loosed also in heaven" (Matthew 16:18-19).

After receiving from Peter a threefold profession of love, Christ commits to him the feeding of His entire flock saying:

"Feed my lambs . . . feed my sheep" (John 21:15-17).

Reminding Peter that Satan was conspiring against all the Apostles, Christ says to Peter:

"But I have prayed for *thee,* that *thy* faith fail not; and *thou,* being once converted, confirm *thy* brethren" (Luke 22:32).

THE POPE IS PETER'S SUCCESSOR

Pope Peter was the first Pope, the first Bishop of Rome, the first visible head of Christ's Church. The successors to the office first held by Peter inherit all the power and authority which Christ conferred upon that office. The long line of pontiffs stretching across 19 centuries, from Peter to Paul VI now gloriously reigning, numbers 263 and constitutes the abstract of the Catholic Church's title to being the one, true Church of Jesus Christ on earth.

BISHOPS ARE THE SUCCESSORS OF THE APOSTLES

Bishops Christ assures the Apostles that He will be with them in their work of teaching all nations unto the end of time, saying to them:

"And behold I am with you all days, even to the consummation of the world" (Matthew 28:20).

The successors of the Apostles are the bishops, consecrated by the Apostles to continue their divinely appointed task of teaching the truths of Christ to all mankind. The power and authority, which every bishop in the Catholic Church possesses, have come to him through a long line of bishops from one of the Apostles who in turn received such powers from Christ Himself.

Priests Priests, commonly called presbyters in the early centuries, are ordained by bishops to carry on the sacred ministry of preaching, pardoning and offering up the Eucharistic Sacrifice.

Luke records the action of Paul and Barnabas in ordaining priests to carry on their work:

"And when they had ordained to them priests in every church, and had prayed with fasting, they commended them to the Lord, in Whom they believed" (Acts 14:22).

THREEFOLD POWER OF PRIESTHOOD

Upon His first priests, Christ confers the threefold power of the priesthood, namely, to preach with authority, to forgive sins, to offer the Eucharistic Sacrifice.

Power of Preaching. "Go ye into the whole world, and preach the gospel to every creature. He that believeth and is baptized, will be saved: but he that believeth not shall be condemned" (Mark 16: 15-16).

Power of Pardoning. "Receive ye the Holy Ghost. Whose sins you shall forgive, they are forgiven them; and whose sins you shall retain, they are retained" (John 20:22-23).

Power of Consecrating. After pronouncing the words of consecration at the Last Supper, thereby changing the bread and wine into His Body and Blood, Christ said to His first priests:

"Do this for a commemoration of Me" (Luke 22:19).

PRIESTHOOD MUST NOT BE USURPED

Christ says to His first priests at the Last Supper:

"You have not chosen Me: but I have chosen you; and have appointed you, that you should go, and should bring forth fruit; and your fruit should remain: that whatsoever you shall ask of the Father in My name, He may give it to you" (John 15:16).

Paul warns against the usurpation of the priestly office, saying:

"For every high priest taken from among men is ordained for

men in the things that appertain to God, that he may offer up gifts and sacrifices for sins. . . . Neither doth any man take the honor to himself, but he that is called by God, as Aaron was" (Hebrews 5:1-4).

THE MARK OF UNITY

The members of Christ's Church are all bound together by the bond of a common faith, are united in the reception of the same sacraments, and all acknowledge the authority of their divinely appointed spiritual leaders, bishops, priests and supreme pontiff.

"There shall be one fold and one shepherd" (John 10:16).

Paul exhorts the Ephesians to be "careful to keep the unity of the Spirit in the bond of peace. One body and one Spirit; as you are called in one hope of your calling. One Lord, one faith and one baptism" (Ephesians 4:3-6).

Paul sounds a similar note to the Galatians, saying:

"But though we, or an angel from heaven, preach a gospel to you besides that which we have preached to you, let him be anathema . . . for I give you to understand, brethren, that the gospel which was preached by me is not according to man. For neither did I receive it of man, nor did I learn it; but by the revelation of Jesus Christ" (Galatians 1:8-12).

CHRIST'S MYSTICAL BODY

Catholic Family   The members of Christ's Church are members of Christ's Mystical Body. Thus Paul says of Christ:

"He is the Head of the body, the Church" (Colossians 1:18).

"So we being many are one body in Christ" (Romans 12:5).

"As the branch cannot bear fruit of itself unless it abide in the vine, so neither can you unless you abide in Me" (John 15:4).

THE PEARL OF GREAT PRICE

Conclusion   The Catholic Church was founded by Jesus Christ in Jerusalem, A.D. 33. He conferred upon it the power to teach all nations all the truths which He taught, and He assured the Church that He is with it all days even to the consummation of the world. Christ chose Peter as the first pope. His successors govern with all the power and authority conferred by Christ upon Peter. The bishops are the successors of the Apostles, and ordain priests to carry on the ministry of preaching, pardoning and offering up the Eucharistic Sacrifice. The members of Christ's Church are members of His Mystical Body, the prolongation of the Incarnation, sharing through grace Christ's divine life. All profess the same faith and acknowledge the same spiritual authority. Membership in the Catholic Church, the one true Church of Jesus Christ on earth, and the observance of its laws and teachings bring you eternal salvation.

BACK HOME AGAIN

So much then for the biblical blueprint of Christ's Church. So much for the evidence of the divine foundation of the Catholic Church and for her authority to teach all mankind in the name of Jesus Christ. Now the time has come for you to *pray* and to *act*. Faith is a gift of God. It requires not only a turning of the eyes of the intellect to the light of divine truth but also a genuflection of the will to God's decree and plan.

God never turns a deaf ear to the prayer of the man who on his knees cries out: "Lord, that I may see!" In response to that moving cry and prayer, God causes His light to shine and stretches forth a hand to lift him to his feet and to guide him aright. Pray then fervently and, as St. Paul says, "Pray without ceasing" (Thessalonians 5:17).

Do not hesitate to call upon a priest; have him explain to you in detail the teachings of the Catholic faith. This he will do gladly and freely; you can be assured of kindness, understanding, and personal interest. Since it is a matter of supreme importance, do not delay a single day. Membership in the Church of Jesus Christ will give you peace of mind and happiness here below, and the faithful observance of her teachings and commandments will assure you happiness for all eternity.

St. Paul has said: "Eye hath not seen, nor ear heard, neither hath it entered into the heart of man, what things God hath prepared for them that love him" (I Corinthians 2:9). Through this little book Christ is calling you, saying, "Come to Me all you who labor and are burdened, and I will give you rest" (Matthew 11:28).